MAKING
CHRISTMAS TABLE
DECORATIONS

Polly Pinder

SEARCH PRESS

First published in Great Britain 2006

Search Press Limited
Wellwood, North Farm Road,
Tunbridge Wells, Kent TN2 3DR

Text copyright © Polly Pinder 2006

Photographs by Storm Studios

Photographs and design copyright © Search Press Ltd. 2006

ISBN 978 1 84448 077 7

The Publishers and author can accept no responsibility for any consequences arising from the information, advice or instructions given in this publication.

Suppliers
If you have difficulty in obtaining any of the materials and equipment mentioned in this book, then please visit the Search Press website for details of suppliers:
www.searchpress.com

Publishers' note
All the step-by-step photographs in this book feature the author, Polly Pinder, demonstrating how to make Christmas table decorations. No models have been used.

Printed in Malaysia by Times Offset (M) Sdn Bhd

Dedicated to my very dear friends Pam and Adrian – for just being there and for the great, sometimes rowdy, Wednesday art, supper and scrabble evenings – Adrian I will beat you yet! And not forgetting their lovely children Gabriel, Rosie and Flora.

Acknowledgements
I would like to thank the good folk of Search Press for their many years of guidance, support and affection, and Storm for these stunning photographs and the sticky buns.

Also the following companies whose products have been used in this book:
Lever Craft Punches
Anita's Art Stamps and Outline Stickers
Woodcare Craft Collections
Stitch and Craft
Habicraft
Whispers Stamps

Page 1
Mix and Match Gift Boxes
I have decorated these to show how useful it is to keep bits and pieces. The embellishments were collected from last year's Christmas crackers. It would have been such a shame to waste them. The gift boxes have been transformed by the addition of gold foliage, green holographic paper, matt gold paper and plum-coloured nail varnish applied to the pearls and diamond settings.

Opposite
Classical Holly Napkin Rings
See page 38.
Spirelli Snowflake Bags
See page 26.

Contents

Introduction 4

Materials 6

Christmas Candle
Shade 10

Copper Trees
Centrepiece 16

Country Carrier
Gift Bag 22

Twirling Holly
Candle Holder 28

Golden Weave
Napkin Rings 34

Star Shine Surprise
Boxes 40

Templates 45

Index 48

Introduction

Many of our Christmas traditions were introduced from Northern Europe during the Victorian era; but I have a feeling that in the darker days before Christmas was celebrated, our ancestors used flowers, leaves and other natural objects to decorate the table for a feast.

Planning the table for various festive meals is the perfect antidote to midwinter blues. Even if things are left to the last minute, there are always simple ideas which can be put together using a few craft items and an assortment of things found around the house. I am an obsessive champion for recycling. Many of the following designs evolved around bits and pieces from the previous year's cards and gift wrap. The perforated metal for the candle shade project on page 10 was rescued from a skip, and the little metal bucket used for the candle holder on page 28 was previously a plant pot. Do save anything that might have possibilities; your imagination can start working at the mere glimpse of any lovely shiny or shimmering thing.

The decorations in this book will brighten up the seasonal table and give some extra delight to family and friends. So, have a wonderful and memorable Christmas.

Polly

Materials

Paper

We really need to thank the producers of paper and card in the craft industry because every year they make available more exciting and sumptuous ranges for our little collections. We can dip into these, experiment with them and use our imaginations to create really beautiful objects. Here are many of the papers used in the following chapters. They include: red, green, gold and silver **self-adhesive holographic paper**; red and green **tissue paper**; **card**, silver **corrugated card** and **glitter card**; **synthetic copper-coloured spun paper**; **banana-leaf handmade paper**; gold and silver **metallic paper**; **strong, matt gold paper**; **scrap paper** to protect your work surface from spray paint and **tracing paper** for transferring designs. The one at the bottom is **draft film**. This can be bought at most art shops and is a perfect medium for diffusing candle light. I have used it for the candle shades on pages 10 to 15.

Beads and wire

Many craft shops now stock varieties of stunning **beads**. They come in so many shapes, sizes, colours and textures; and are made from different material – glass, paper, wood, plastic and resin; some even have specks of gold flake embedded in them.

Companies are also producing different colours and thicknesses of **wire** for our crafts; I can remember having to use fuse wire not so long ago. **Florist's metal ribbon** is very malleable; I have used it to make a bow and tube cover on page 21. I found the **perforated metal sheeting** in a skip. It is used in radiator covers and can be bought from most hardware stores. It is surprisingly easy to cut with a pair of old scissors.

Headpins are long, blunt pins used in the jewellery industry. You will be able to get them from most bead shops.

Embellishments

All sorts of things can be used to embellish your Christmas table decorations. Lovely **ribbons** and **bows**, metallic and decorative **threads**; **gold-painted berries** and **pine cones**; **wire mesh hearts,** often woven with combinations of very narrow ribbon and sparkling seed beads; pieces cut from the stems of **artificial flowers**; coloured **feathers, string, packing straw** and **pipe cleaners**. In the spirit of recycling, do not forget the little things which adorned last year's presents and crackers; they can easily be adapted and enhanced to make new embellishments for this year.

Blanks

These are the objects used in the book as a basis for the decorations. Some of them can be found in most kitchens: various sized glasses, tea lights, loose bases from cake tins (not illustrated but used for the candle holder on page 32) and in the garden shed, little galvanised buckets and plant pots. The small gift bags and covered or blank boxes can be bought from craft shops and some stationers. The gold, red and blue candles are in most stores at this time of the year. Gold crockery is becoming increasingly popular. The lovely, large resin plates are often used as place mats and there are lots of ceramic dishes and bowls, one of which I have used as a stand for the centrepiece on page 21. This little wreath was bought at my local craft store. I pressed it down to form a flatter base for the Copper Trees Centrepiece on page 19. I found a set of the 'larger than usual' cork drinks mats in one of those wonderful stores which sell lots of unrelated things very cheaply. They had cartoon characters on the other side but they did not show with the mats turned upside down.

Other equipment

It really is easy and preferable to use a **cutting mat** when using your **metal ruler** and **craft knife**. It should last for years and no matter how much pressure you exert, the mat will heal up again. Do not forget to use your metal ruler when cutting, as a plastic one will not last long once the blade has nicked into it. A **plastic ruler** can be used for measuring.

You will also need an HB **pencil**, an **eraser** and a **black felt pen** for the Twirling Holly Candle Holder project on page 28.

You will need a few pairs of **scissors**: one or two pairs of fairly small, good quality sharp, pointed ones; a pair of deckle-edged for cutting snowflakes and an old pair for cutting thin wire. The **wire cutters** are needed for cutting any thick wire and the little **round-nosed pliers** are useful for bending and curling the wire.

I have used three kinds of sewing needle for the various materials (see the list at the beginning of each project): a **tapestry needle**, which has a blunt end; a **darning needle**, which is strong, long and sharp; and a **beading needle** which is very fine and sharp. A **thimble** is useful for pushing the fine beading needle through stiff card, as in the Copper Trees Centrepiece project on page 16. The **drinking straws** are used as tree trunks for the same project.

Glue is one of the most important items in the crafter's cupboard. I have used a **glue stick, clear all-purpose adhesive, sticky tape** and **double-sided tape** in three different widths. The **stapler** comes in handy when glue or tape are not strong enough.

Craft punches and an ordinary **office hole punch** are used in three of the projects and in many of the other decorations shown.

The **rubber stamps, inkpad** and **glitter** were used for the Simple Stamped Bags shown on page 27.

Nail varnish, particularly the pearlescent type, is really good for radically changing the appearance of a project. **Acrylic paint**, which becomes waterproof when dry, is equally useful. Always rinse your **paintbrushes** thoroughly when using the paint.

Craft stickers and **invisible thread** were used to make the Crystal Stars Candle Shade on page 15.

Fine horticultural **sand** can be bought from most garden centres. I have used it to secure things which need to stand upright in containers.

Gold and silver **spray paints** are used to decorate projects. The **decorating mask** is important and should always be worn while spraying, near an open window or door if possible.

Opposite
Gold and silver spray paint and a decorating mask; office hole punch; stapler; craft punches; clear all-purpose glue and glue stick; metal and plastic rulers; drinking straws; deckle-edged, ordinary, sharp, pointed and old scissors; wire cutters and round-nosed pliers; invisible thread, tapestry, darning and beading needles and a thimble; craft knife and cutting mat; paintbrushes, pencil and felt-tipped pen; eraser; craft stickers; double-sided tape in different widths; glitter; sticky tape; rubber stamps and inkpad; acrylic paint; nail varnish and sand.

CHRISTMAS CANDLE SHADE

You will need

Brass coloured perforated metal sheeting 100 x 235mm (4 x 9¼in)

Bobbin of fine gold-coloured wire and tapestry needle

Old scissors, sharp-pointed scissors, craft knife and cutting mat

A4 sheet each of red and green self-adhesive holographic paper

Gold berry and leaf decoration on wire

A4 sheet each of red and green tissue paper

Draft film, 100 x 205mm (4 x 8in)

Small straight-sided glass tumbler, 60mm (2½in) in diameter and 85mm (3¼in) tall

Tea lights

Metal ruler and pencil

Sticky tape and glue stick

Decorative shades are a lovely way of enhancing ordinary tea lights. Each tea light is placed in a glass tumbler, then the tumbler is put into a decorated or perforated tube from which limited light is emitted. The outer form of this candle shade project is perforated metal sheeting, which I found in a skip – it had been used as a radiator cover. You can buy it in hardware stores, and it is soft enough to cut with old scissors. The little gold berries were bought as a larger bunch from my local craft shop, as were the holographic papers. The measurements here are dependent on the size of your tumbler. Remember that you must never leave a candle unattended.

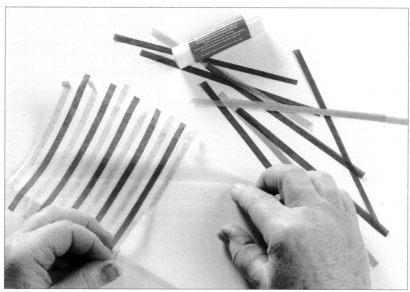

1. Using your craft knife and metal ruler, cut the red and green tissue paper into 5 x 130mm (¼ x 5in) strips. Using the glue stick, stick the strips firmly on to the draft film, leaving a 5mm (¼in) gap between each strip. Trim the edges flush with the film.

2. Attach half the width of a length of sticky tape along one edge (on the side where the strips have not been stuck). Bring the other edge round and press it on to the other half of the sticky tape, so that the tube is joined from the inside.

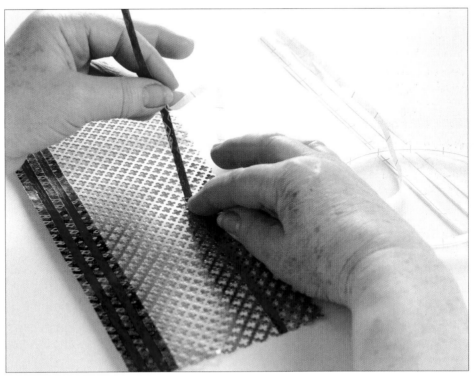

3. Cut the holographic paper into six lengths, three of each colour, measuring 5 x 235mm (¼ x 9¼in). Peel off the backing and stick five round the base of the metal and one near the top at the same height as the glass tumbler.

4. Curl the metal round the glass; this will help to achieve the tubular shape.

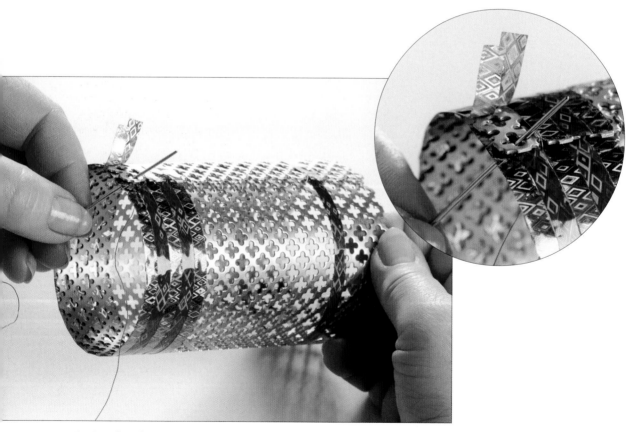

5. Overlap the edges by 10mm (½in) and neatly sew them together using a tapestry needle to thread the wire in and out of the perforations. Temporarily lift the strips of holographic paper so that you can reach the perforations on the top overlap.

6. Carefully thread the berry sprays into the perforations, pushing the wire stem in through the front, then out, then back in again. Press the wire stem against the inside of the shade.

Tip

Be careful how you pick up the candle shade. Hold on to the bottom of the tumbler or it will fall out of the shade.

7. Slide the striped draft film liner inside the metal shade, seam against seam, being careful not to catch it on the wire stems. Carefully put the glass tumbler containing the candle inside the completed shade.

Tip

It is usually difficult to light the candle while it is in the tumbler. So, light the candle first, pinch the side of the candle's metal container with your pliers and carefully place it in the tumbler.

The finished candle shade. Light is magical, especially when it is reflected on shiny surfaces or transformed into rays coming from tiny apertures. These decorations will add a warm glow to the Christmas table.

Real Snowflakes and Crystal Stars

The images on the green candle shades are taken from magnified photographs of real snowflakes, which you can scan from this book (see page 47). Draw the outline of your candle shade on the computer screen and place the scanned snowflakes, then you may want to change the background colour to one of your own choice.

In the white draft film shade, the crystal beads reflect light coming through star apertures. Each aperture was made by positioning an outline sticker, then cutting away the film inside the star. The beads are held in place by short lengths of invisible nylon thread which are caught by craft sticker stars.

COPPER TREES CENTREPIECE

Appreciative comments about the beautiful centrepiece, together with a glass of mulled wine, are always a good start to the Christmas meal. The trees for this project are made from orange card covered with a synthetic paper which has a look of finely spun frosted silk. It can be bought, together with the card, wreath and miniature plant pots, from most craft shops. I bought the cork mat from a hardware store but you could use a piece of sturdy card – just draw round a dish. Wonderful beads of all sizes, shapes and colours are available from specialist shops and mail order stockists.

1. Transfer the tree shape and circle on page 46 on to the orange card three times. Cut them out. Attach pieces of double-sided tape to the flaps on the circles, then use your craft knife to cut the central holes. Bend all the flaps down.

16

2. Attach pieces of double-sided tape down the sides of each tree shape. Press spun paper on top and then cut away the excess paper. Put pieces of double-sided tape round the edges of the cork mat, attach the spun paper and trim away the edges.

3. Use the copper-coloured thread and beading needle to sew beads on to the tree shape randomly, including strands of little seed beads. Knot each bead or strand securely at the back before going on to the next one. If you do not knot each bead at the back, when the shape is curled into a tree, the thread will becomes loose and the beads will dangle.

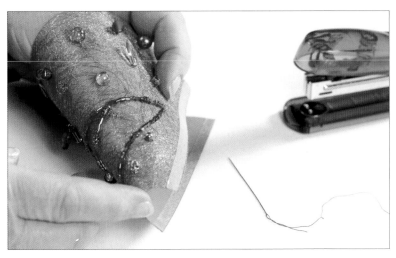

4. Stick strips of double-sided tape down each side of the beaded shapes, one at the back and one at the front. Remove the backing and carefully curl the shape round, sticking the two sides together. Secure with a couple of stitches at the top and staples in the middle and at the bottom of the seam.

5. Remove the backing from the double-sided tape on the tabs around each circle. Place a circle inside the base of each tree shape and press the tabs to secure them.

6. Place a piece of double-sided tape in the bottom of each pot. Give each pot two coats of green acrylic paint. Wash your brush immediately because acrylic paint dries hard very quickly.

7. Make four 20mm (¾in) slits at the bottom of a drinking straw and press the cut pieces outwards. Position the splayed ends on to the double-sided tape in a plant pot and pour sand up to the rim. Repeat with the other plant pots.

8. Cut nine strips of double-sided tape 5 x 25mm (¼ x 1in) and three 5 x 50mm (¼ x 2in). Position three small ones, crossing each other, on the top of each tree to cover the hole. Remove the backing after positioning each one. Stick the three longer pieces round the top edge.

9. Transfer the small star on page 46 on to the back of the glitter card twelve times. Cut the stars out and bend the points upwards. Turn them over and attach a piece of double-sided tape to one point of each star. Remove the backing and stick four sides together.

Tip

When you need to transfer an image many times (the twelve stars for example) it is easier to transfer one on to a piece of card, cut it out and then carefully draw round it twelve times.

10. Slide the trees on to the straws in the pots.

11. Carefully position the stars on top. Flatten the wreath to accommodate the mat then place the three pots on top. The wreath, mat and pots could be permanently attached using clear all-purpose glue if you wish.

Opposite

The finished centrepiece. Time is needed to make these little trees but you could always listen to a good Christmas play while sewing on the gorgeous beads. The spun paper is very easy to work with and has a stunning effect.

Shimmering Tree Centrepiece

This tree goes with the woven napkin rings on page 37. The weaving is stuck to the tube from a roll of cling film. The tree is made from two bunches of gold wire which I bought from one of those great shops that sell everything for virtually nothing. I made the gold stars, threaded some seed beads, punched out snowflakes and hung some little jewels and baubles.

All Wired Up Centrepiece

I bought two rolls of this wonderful wire at my local florist, where it is sold as florist's metal ribbon. The container is a cocoa tin covered with pearlescent paper and then the wire. The feathers, berries and gold cones were bought at a craft shop and having folded the wire up to make a ribbon bow, I filled the tin with sand, put everything in, then stood it on a little gold plate.

COUNTRY CARRIER GIFT BAG

You will need

A4 sheet of textured handmade paper

Seven 250mm (10in) strands of rough string

A tiny spray of artificial berries

An artificial holly leaf

Fine packing straw

Craft knife, metal ruler and cutting mat

Double-sided tape

Scissors

Office hole punch

Tracing paper and pencil

These little bags can contain any lovely delight, perhaps a small, personal gift for each guest. The bags can be bought at most craft stores and some greetings card shops. They can be decorated using stamped images or spirelli designs (see pages 26–27), quilled shapes, beading or even stars and snowflakes punched from last year's Christmas cards.

It is not difficult to make little bags yourself – there is a template on page 45. I have chosen a heavily textured banana-leaf handmade paper which, combined with the string and packing straw, give a natural, country look. If you can not find artificial holly leaves, you can always cut one from some stiff green paper, using the template on page 45.

1. Transfer the bag template on to the back of your paper. Cut it out and indent the fold lines using the handle of your craft knife.

2. Fold all the creases, starting with the top narrow flap. Slide the folded top into the hole punch and make the four holes where indicated.

3. Attach pieces of double-sided tape to the two larger flaps and to the back of the side flap as shown. Peel off the backing.

4. First stick the two sides together with the flap inside. Then tuck the small bottom flaps in and stick the larger ones on top. Press from the inside to ensure a firm attachment.

5. Knot three strands of string together and plait them firmly.

6. Thread the plait through two holes on one side of the bag, then knot the ends on the inside of the bag. Make another plait with three more strands and attach it in the same way.

7. Wind the remaining strand into a flat circle. Carefully, without allowing it to spring away, press it on to a piece of double-sided tape. Trim off any excess tape.

8. Remove the backing from the wound string and attach the berry spray and holly leaf behind the string. Put another piece of double-sided tape behind all three items and press it securely on to the bag.

9. Place a handful of packing straw into the bag, together with the chosen gift.

Tip

You could use a tiny spray of fresh red berries and a real holly leaf, or perhaps variegated ivy instead of holly to avoid injury.

Opposite

These little gift bags are really easy to make. I have used a highly textured, handmade banana-leaf paper, but an ordinary strong, brown wrapping paper would look just as good. I have put two stitches through the tops of the handles to keep them together, but this is unnecessary if you feel that your guest will want quick access to the contents!

Spirelli Snowflake Bags

Sometimes it is nice to deviate from the traditional Christmas colours and introduce something new, like this lovely purple holographic paper. The little snowflakes were cut with a craft punch from sparkly card. The large spirelli snowflake was cut out using deckle-edged scissors. Metallic purple thread was used to wind round the pieces of flake which were then stuck together.

Simple Stamped Bags

I bought these and the purple bags from a greetings card shop. The holographic papers are irresistible; they have such a magical effect, showing all the colours of the rainbow. The idea is to have a different Christmas image on each little bag. The image was stamped using silver sparkle embossing powder. The red pearlescent circles were cut from last year's Christmas carrier bag. I used two stitches to secure the little bow and the bag filling is red tissue paper.

TWIRLING HOLLY CANDLE HOLDER

You will need

Galvanised bucket 80mm (3in) high and 90mm (3½in) in diameter, and fine sand to fill it

Red candle 100mm (4in) tall

Round red glass beads, red cotton thread and a needle

A5 sheet of corrugated silver card

A5 sheet of silver paper

A5 sheet of red self-adhesive holographic paper

Piece of plain card 80mm (3in) square

Roll of sturdy silver-coloured wire and wire cutters

Pencil, tracing paper and black felt pen

Small, sharp, pointed scissors

Double-sided tape

Although candles are used more frequently now, as an aid to relaxation and to create a romantic atmosphere, there is still a particular magic about the flickering light of a Christmas candle.

The decidedly unromantic galvanised bucket used for this project was found gathering dust and cobwebs in my greenhouse. It had been home to a cactus until the plant grew too large. I like the slight craziness of this concept – twirling holly, bouncing gently at the least movement; and lots of shiny red beads to suggest juicy berries. The narrow border of holographic paper round the leaves gives a wonderful sparkle when the candle is lit.

Do be sure that the leaves are all bending away from the candle flame and never leave any of the candles in this book unattended, particularly when there are children about.

1. Transfer the holly leaves on page 45 on to the piece of plain card. Cut them out to make templates. Lay the smallest one on the front of the corrugated card and, using the felt pen, draw round it seven times. It is easier to cut the holly if you first cut each one out roughly to separate it from the others. Cut the corrugated paper from the front. If you cut from the back, you will tear the silver on the front.

2. Remove the backing from the red holographic paper and stick the silver paper in its place, so that they are back to back. Lay the larger holly template on the silver side and draw round it seven times. Cut out each holly leaf, trying to cut within the black line.

3. Stick a piece of double-sided tape on the back of a corrugated leaf. Attach it to a red leaf. Stick another piece of tape on the back of the red leaf then stick it on the front of the bucket, at an angle as shown.

4. Using the wire cutters, cut six pieces of wire of varying lengths starting from 280mm (11in). Stick a piece of double-sided tape down the centre front of each red leaf, then down the centre back of each corrugated leaf.

5. Remove the backing and lay a piece of wire on the double-sided tape on a red leaf. Carefully lay the corrugated leaf on top and press together firmly. Repeat with the other leaves.

Tip

The wire used for making decorations is usually fairly soft; if you do not have wire cutters, you can use old scissors.

6. Thread three beads on to each wire. To make a spring, start 80mm (3in) from the end of the wire and wrap it smoothly round your thumb, but not too tightly. Slide the spring off your thumb: it can be now be stretched out or pushed tighter.

7. Pour sand into the bucket, leaving roughly a depth of one bead at the top. Push the candle firmly into the centre. Use the needle to thread enough beads onto the cotton to wind once round the base of the candle. Knot the cotton securely, then position the string of beads round the base. Put some loose beads on top to disturb the uniformity.

8. Push the holly springs into the sand and twist them carefully until the arrangement is balanced and to your liking. The springs can be removed and adjusted if required.

Opposite

The finished candle holder. The silver colour scheme creates a fresh, modern look and makes a change from the usual Christmas gold. The fine sand which supports the candle and springs can be bought from garden centres.

Snowflakes and Ice Cubes
I could not resist the magnificently detailed silver card that forms the curved part of this candle holder. I made a base from cardboard, covered it with silver paper, edged it with gold and added gold outline stickers. I backed the silver card with silver paper, then used double-sided tape to stick it on to the base – it curved naturally because the base width was narrower than the card. The silver backing paper reflects the gold outline stickers on the base. The glass cube candle holders are stuck with clear all-purpose glue.

Opposite
Christmas Cocktails
I bought these cocktail glasses from a charity shop. Upside down, they make perfect holders for the square blue candles. The base is made from two baking tin bases, covered with metallic and holographic papers and stuck together with double-sided tape. The most difficult thing was trying to keep the metallic straw in the glasses – it has a mind of its own. Everything can be reclaimed after the festivities.

GOLDEN WEAVE NAPKIN RINGS

Coordinating your table decorations creates a sense of visual unity and cohesion. These woven napkin rings go with the Shimmering Tree Centrepiece on page 20. In order to achieve the lovely golden weave, I gathered together absolutely anything that had a hint of gold – old greeting cards and Christmas crackers, pipe cleaners, thread, cord, ribbon, holographic paper and bits of packaging. The main part of the ring is made from a sturdy matt gold paper. The ends of each threaded strip are cut obliquely, or cut and curled, or frayed. It is lovely to watch the different golden textures and shades grow as you weave them through.

You will need

To make one ring:

Strong, matt gold paper 50 x 180mm (2 x 7in)

Strips of gold paper, card, thread, cord, pipe cleaner and ribbon roughly 5 x 70mm (¼ x 2¾in)

Gold, self-adhesive holographic paper

Fine gold wire

Cardboard tube from a kitchen towel roll

Snowflake craft punch

Craft knife, scissors, old scissors for cutting wire and cutting mat

Double-sided tape and sticky tape

Pencil and metal ruler

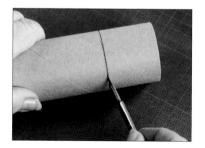

1. Using your pencil and ruler, measure and draw a line round the tube 45mm (1¾in) from the edge. Then, using your craft knife and a sawing motion, cut the section off.

2. Turn the matt gold paper over. Draw lines 20mm (¾in) from the top and bottom edges. Then draw nine lines 5mm (⅜in) apart between the top and bottom lines. Carefully cut along the vertical lines.

Tip

If you have found some interesting gold paper which is too flimsy to use either as the ring or the strips, simply stick some ordinary cartridge or typing paper on the back to make it firmer.

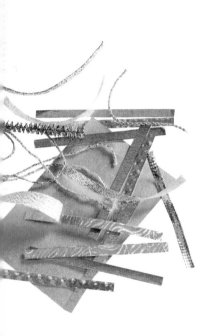

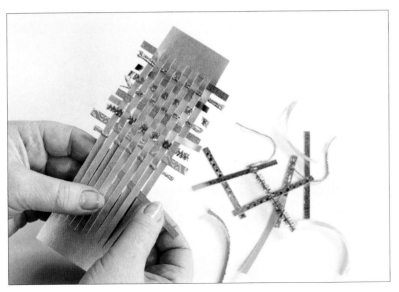

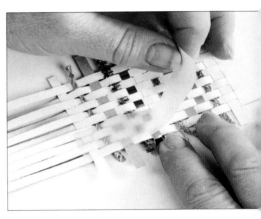

3. Start to thread the various strips of gold alternately through the matt gold bands.

4. When you have reached half way, turn the weaving over. Firmly push each side in so that all the bands are as close as possible. Secure each side with a piece of sticky tape. Continue threading, then tighten and secure the remaining half in the same way.

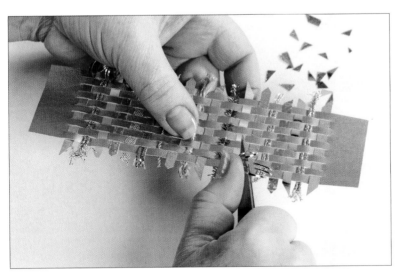

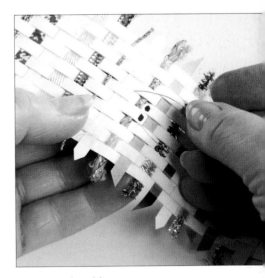

5. With the front of the weaving facing you, cut some of the strip ends diagonally or to a point, curl others round your scissors as shown and fray the ends of any cord or ribbon.

6. Using the old scissors, cut three pieces of wire 90mm (3½in) long. Mark the centre of the weaving on the back then thread each wire through so that both ends stick out of the front. Secure the wires at the back with a piece of sticky tape.

7. Straighten the wires at the front so that they stand up as shown.

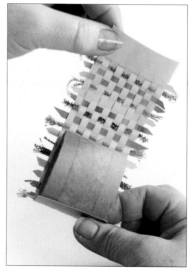

8. Attach a piece of double-sided tape round the centre of the cardboard tube. Then attach another piece to the top back border of the weaving. Carefully but firmly wrap the weaving round the tube. The weaving should overlap the tube slightly at both sides.

9. Punch twelve snowflakes from the gold holographic paper. Remove the backing and using the tip of your craft knife, carefully attach two snowflakes, sticky side to sticky side, to the tip of each wire.

Opposite
The finished napkin rings. These richly woven decorations can be used at the table together with the matching Shimmering Tree Centrepiece (page 20).

Classical Holly Napkin Rings

Here I chose red and green glitter card and a stiff, textured paper, the same colour as the napkins. A single craft punch combined the holly with a decorative border and an office hole punch made the gold and silver holographic circles and the holes through which the metallic ribbon was threaded.

Beads and Berries Napkin Rings

These were so simple to make. I used last year's Christmas crackers to make the box-like ring, then strung all the varying sized beads on thin wire, wrapped the beaded wire round the rings, then wired the leaves and berries on to each end.

STAR SHINE SURPRISE BOXES

You will need

To make one box:

Star-shaped blank box

Gold and silver spray paint, mask and scrap paper

Gold and silver seed beads

Fifteen silver wire headpins and 150mm (6in) of silver wire

Silver glitter card, 80 x 130mm (3 x 5in)

Sheet each of self-adhesive gold and silver metallic paper, 50 x100mm (2 x 4in)

Scissors, craft knife and cutting mat

Tracing paper, pencil and metal ruler

Small and medium star craft punches

Double-sided tape, sticky tape and clear all-purpose glue

Little paintbrush or wooden skewer

Round-nosed pliers, wire cutters and darning needle

These little boxes have the same function as the gift bags; they contain nice surprises for your Christmas guests. It is a good idea, if possible, to make them coordinate with other table decorations such as the centrepiece or napkin rings.

The blank boxes are usually a natural brown colour and need covering or painting. They come in several different shapes and are available from craft stores. I have used a star-shaped box for this project and sprayed the lid gold and the box silver. The rays of star shine are headpins, which you can buy from most bead shops, with tiny beads threaded on.

1. Cover your working surface with scrap paper to protect it, put your mask on and open a window. Position the box and lid then spray the box silver and the lid gold.

2. When the box and lid are dry, punch out approximately ten medium and ten small gold stars, then thirteen medium and eighteen small silver stars from the self-adhesive paper. Remove the backing with the tip of your craft knife and stick the gold stars on the box and the silver stars on the lid.

3. Transfer the large star on page 47 on to the back of the glitter card, twice. Cut the stars out using your craft knife, ruler and cutting mat or sharp, pointed scissors. Using the knife, cut a 5mm (¼in) hole in the centre of one star.

4. Stick a small piece of double-sided tape on to the back of the leftover glitter card, then punch out a small star. Position a medium gold star and the small glitter star in the centre of the other large star.

5. Wind the wire round the paintbrush handle to make a spring. Pull a little of the end out and attach it to the centre underside of the large glitter star without a hole, using a piece of double-sided tape. Add a piece of sticky tape to secure it firmly.

6. Thread ten mixed beads each on to two headpins and fourteen on to another. Position the headpin with most beads in the centre then use your round-nosed pliers to hold the pins and twist tightly so that the three are held together. Repeat four more times so that you have a total of five star shine rays.

7. Using the wire cutters, cut the ends from each of the five beaded rays, leaving about 5mm (¼in) of twisted pins.

8. Place the rays round the spring as shown. Attach them using double-sided tape underneath and sticky tape on top, as for the spring.

9. Lay the completed star face down, squeeze a little clear glue round the centre then slide the other glitter star face down over the spring. Position it firmly making sure that the star points correspond with the beaded rays.

10. When the glue is completely dry, place a piece of double-sided tape on the inside centre of the box lid. Use the darning needle to pierce a hole in the centre. Push the end of the spring through and press it on to the double-sided tape, then cover it with sticky tape to secure it.

Opposite
The finished boxes. There is something undeniably cheeky about things wobbling on a little spring. This gorgeous star is attached to a handmade spring and vibrates gently at the slightest movement. I am going to use these Star Shine Surprise Boxes for a special Christmas Eve dinner party and put a delicious home-made chocolate in each one.

Yuletide Love Boxes

These are flat-pack boxes that you can buy from greetings card shops and stationers. I used invisible thread to sew the lovely mixed beads to the wire mesh hearts and stuck the hearts on to the boxes with clear all-purpose glue. The folded ribbon is secured in place with double-sided tape and a tiny punched heart has been stuck to the flat part of the ribbon, emphasising the love theme.

Templates

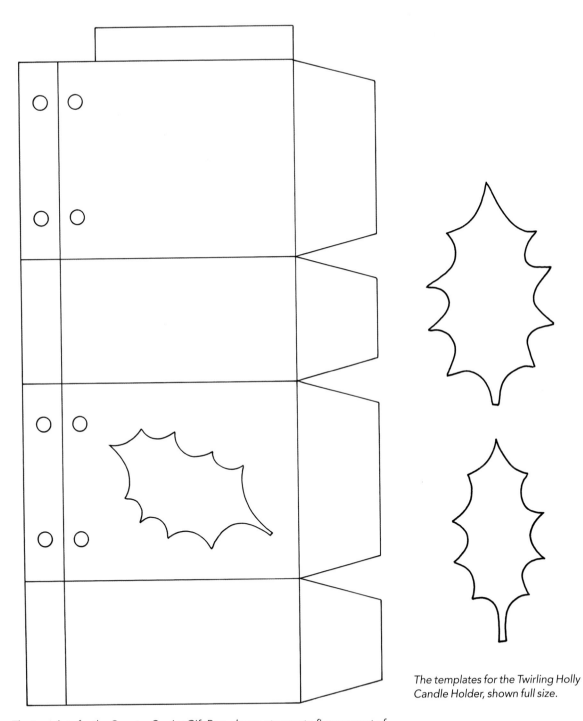

The template for the Country Carrier Gift Bag, shown at seventy-five per cent of actual size. Enlarge it to 133 per cent on a photocopier.

The templates for the Twirling Holly Candle Holder, shown full size.

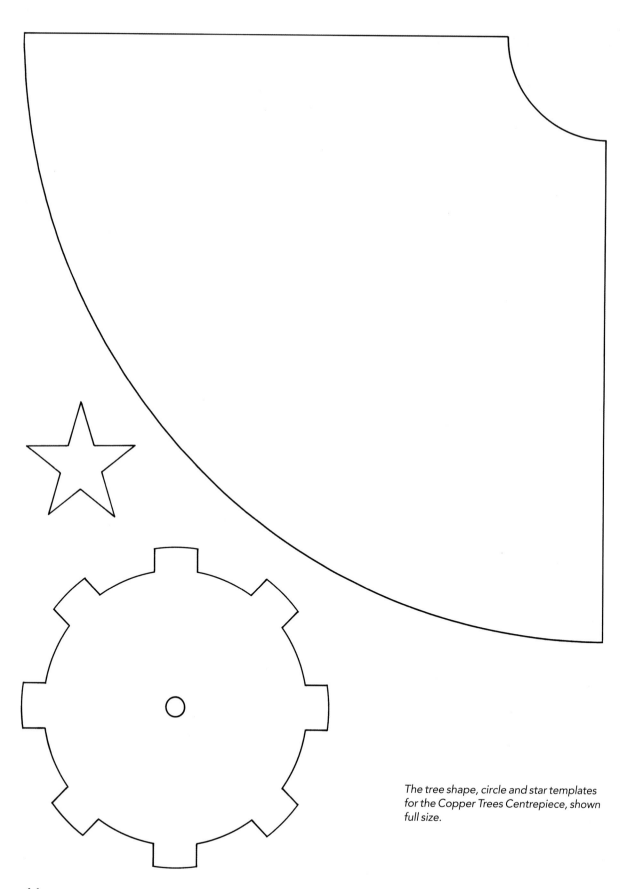

The tree shape, circle and star templates for the Copper Trees Centrepiece, shown full size.

These photographs of real snowflakes can be scanned from this page and used to make the snowflake candle shades shown on page 15.

The template for the Star Shine Surprise Box, shown full size.

Index

acrylic paint 8, 16, 17

beads 6, 7, 16, 17, 18, 20, 30, 39, 40, 41, 44
blank boxes 7, 40
bucket 4, 7, 29, 30

candle 7, 13, 28, 30
candle holder 4, 7, 8, 28–33, 45
candle shade 4, 6, 10–15, 47
card 6, 16, 18, 28
  corrugated 6, 28
  glitter 6, 16, 18, 38, 40, 41
centrepiece 7, 16–21, 34, 36, 40, 46
craft punches 8, 26, 34, 38, 40
craft stickers 8, 15

draft film 6, 10, 13

embellishments
  bows 7, 21, 27
  feathers 7, 21
  packing straw 7, 22, 24
  pipe cleaners 7, 34
  ribbons 7, 34, 35, 38, 44
  string 7, 22, 23, 24
  threads 7, 16, 17, 26, 28, 34, 44
  wire mesh hearts 7, 44

flowers 4, 7

gift bags 7, 22–7, 45

headpins 6, 40, 41

napkin rings 20, 34–39, 40

paper
  banana-leaf handmade 6, 22, 24
  metallic 6, 40
  self-adhesive holographic 6, 10, 28, 34
  spun 6, 16, 17, 18
  tissue 6, 10, 27
  tracing 6, 28, 40
perforated metal 4, 6, 10
plant pot 4, 7, 16, 18

sand 8, 16, 18, 21, 28, 30
snowflakes 8, 15, 20, 22, 26, 33, 34, 36, 47
spirelli 22, 26

spray paints 8, 40
star 22, 40–44, 46
surprise boxes 40–44, 47

tea lights 7, 10

weaving 20, 34, 35, 36
wire 6, 8, 12, 13, 20, 21, 28, 29, 30, 34, 35, 36, 39, 40, 41, 42
  florist's metal ribbon 6, 21
wreath 7, 16, 18